SWITZERLAND

WORLD ADVENTURES

BY STEFFI CAVELL-CLARKE

BookLife

©2018
BookLife Publishing
King's Lynn
Norfolk PE30 4LS

A catalogue record for this
book is available from the
British Library.

ISBN: 978-1-78637-395-3

Written by:
Steffi Cavell-Clarke

Edited by:
Kirsty Holmes

Designed by:
Jasmine Pointer

*All facts, statistics, web addresses and URLs in this book were verified as valid and accurate at time of writing.
No responsibility for any changes to external websites or references can be accepted by either the author or publisher.*

SWITZERLAND
WORLD ADVENTURES

CONTENTS

Words in **bold** can be found in the glossary on page 24.

WHERE IS SWITZERLAND?

Switzerland is a **landlocked** country found in Europe between France, Germany, Italy and Austria.

BERN

The capital city of Switzerland is Bern.

The **population** of Switzerland is over 8 million.
Many people live in the capital city.

THE SWISS ALPS

Switzerland is known for its high mountains and large lakes. The Alps is a mountain range that crosses the country.

Winters in Switzerland are long and snowy in the mountains, while the **valleys** often have fog and rain.

CLOTHING

Most people in Switzerland wear **modern** and comfortable clothing. Sometimes, people wear **traditional** clothing too.

EMBROIDERY

A lot of traditional Swiss clothing has embroidery, which has a bright, colourful design.

RELIGION

CHURCH

The religion with the most followers in Switzerland is Christianity. The Christian place of **worship** is a church. Many Christians visit a church every Sunday for prayer.

Some people follow different religions. There are many people in Switzerland that do not follow any religion.

PEOPLE WHO DO NOT FOLLOW A RELIGION ARE CALLED ATHEISTS.

FOOD

FONDUE

A traditional Swiss dish is the cheese fondue, which is a large bowl of melted cheese that bread is dipped into.

Switzerland is well known around the world for its cheese. Some types of Swiss cheeses have lots of holes in them.

Emmental is a type of Swiss cheese.

AT SCHOOL

In Switzerland, children learn how to read and write in school. They also study subjects such as science, geography and history.

Children in Switzerland go to a school that teaches in the language they speak at home. This is either German, French or Italian.

AT HOME

APARTMENTS

Lots of people live in apartments.

Many people in Switzerland live in **urban** areas, such as towns and cities. Zurich is the largest city in Switzerland.

There are lots of other people who live in villages and towns in the **countryside**, where there are many fields, forests and lakes.

FAMILIES

Many children in Switzerland live with their parents and **siblings** at home. They may also live with other family members, such as their grandparents.

Swiss families like to get together to celebrate special occasions such as weddings and birthdays. They often celebrate by eating special food and singing songs.

CHRISTMAS IN SWITZERLAND IS VERY FESTIVE, AND THERE IS OFTEN SNOW!

SPORT

Football and ice hockey are some of the most popular sports in Switzerland. Many people also enjoy cycling, swimming and snowboarding.

SNOWBOARD

SKIS

Many people from other countries visit Switzerland to go skiing. They slide down snow-covered hills with skis attached to their feet.

FUN FACTS

Yodelling is a form of singing which was used to **communicate** from one hill to another. Many people believe that it began in the Alps in Switzerland.

JOHANNA SPYRI

Heidi has been read by millions of children around the world.

Heidi is a famous book for children that was written in 1881 by a Swiss author, Johanna Spyri. The book is about the life of a young girl living in the Swiss Alps.

GLOSSARY

communicate   share news or ideas with others

countryside   natural or farmed areas of land

landlocked   a country surrounded by land

modern   something from present or recent times

population   number of people living in a place

siblings   brothers and sisters

traditional   ways of behaving that have been done for a long time

urban   a town or city

valleys   low areas of land between hills or mountains

worship   a religious act such as praying

INDEX

Photocredits: Abbreviations: l-left, r-right, b-bottom, t-top, c-centre, m-middle.
All images are courtesy of Shutterstock.com, unless stated otherwise.

Front Cover, 24 – Aleksey Klints. 2 – Alex Tor. 3 – Tatyana Vyc. 4 – T. Lesia. 5 – Boris Stroujko. 6 – Fedor Selivanov. 7 – Natali Glado. 8 – Anna Nahabed. 9 – Pincasso. 10 – canadastock. 11br – In Green. 12 – gorillaimages. 13 – Tim UR. 14 – Anna Nahabed. 15 – ESB Professional. 16 – Blue Jacaranda. 17 – Peter Wey. 18 – Tomsickova Tatyana. 19 – Mihai-Bogdan Lazar. 20 – gorillaimages. 21 – FamVeld. 22 – Sandra Foyt. 23tr – By Rudolf Münger scan by: Adrian Michael – Privatbesitz, Public Domain, https://commons.wikimedia.org/w/index.php?curid=1071324. 23bl – By upload by Adrian Michael – Regine Schindler: Johanna Spyri – Spurensuche, Pendo Verlag, Zürich 1997, Public Domain, https://commons.wikimedia.org/w/index.php?curid=7135546